No More Racism

Freedom is never given, it is WON.
-A. Philip Randolph

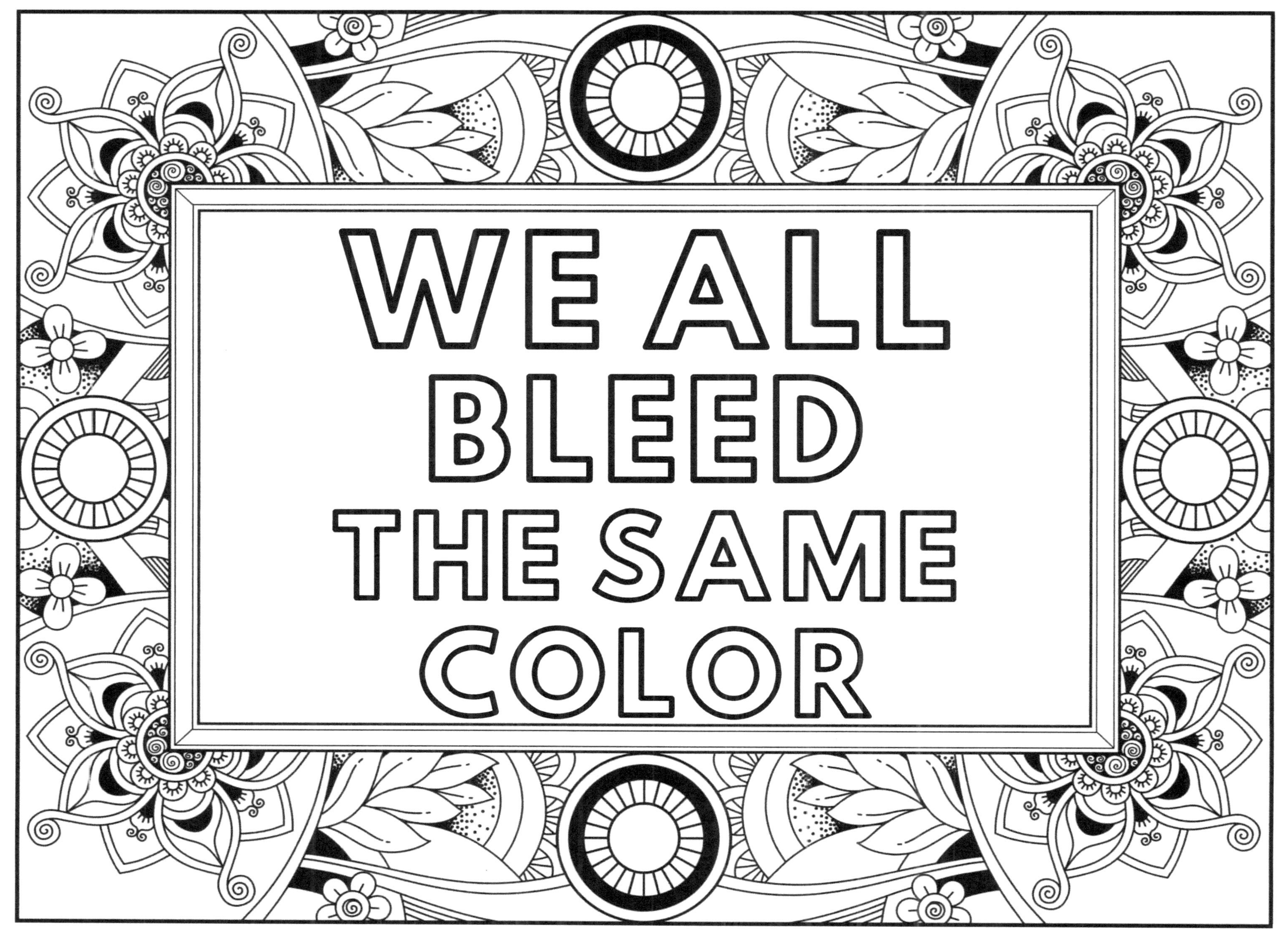

WE ALL
BLEED
THE SAME
COLOR

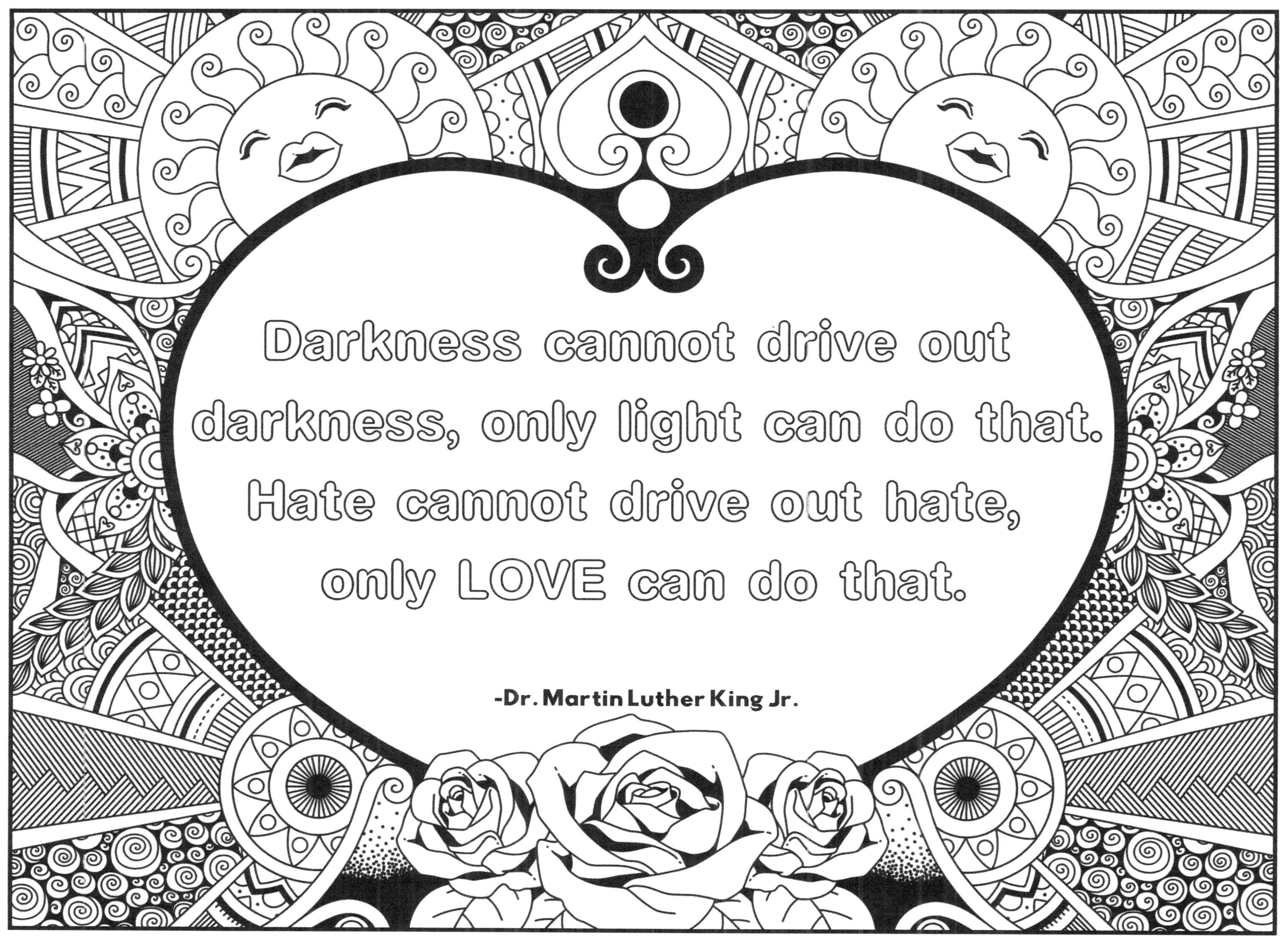

Darkness cannot drive out darkness, only light can do that. Hate cannot drive out hate, only LOVE can do that.
-Dr. Martin Luther King Jr.

Diversity
is the
Future

DO WHAT IS RIGHT
NOT WHAT IS EASY

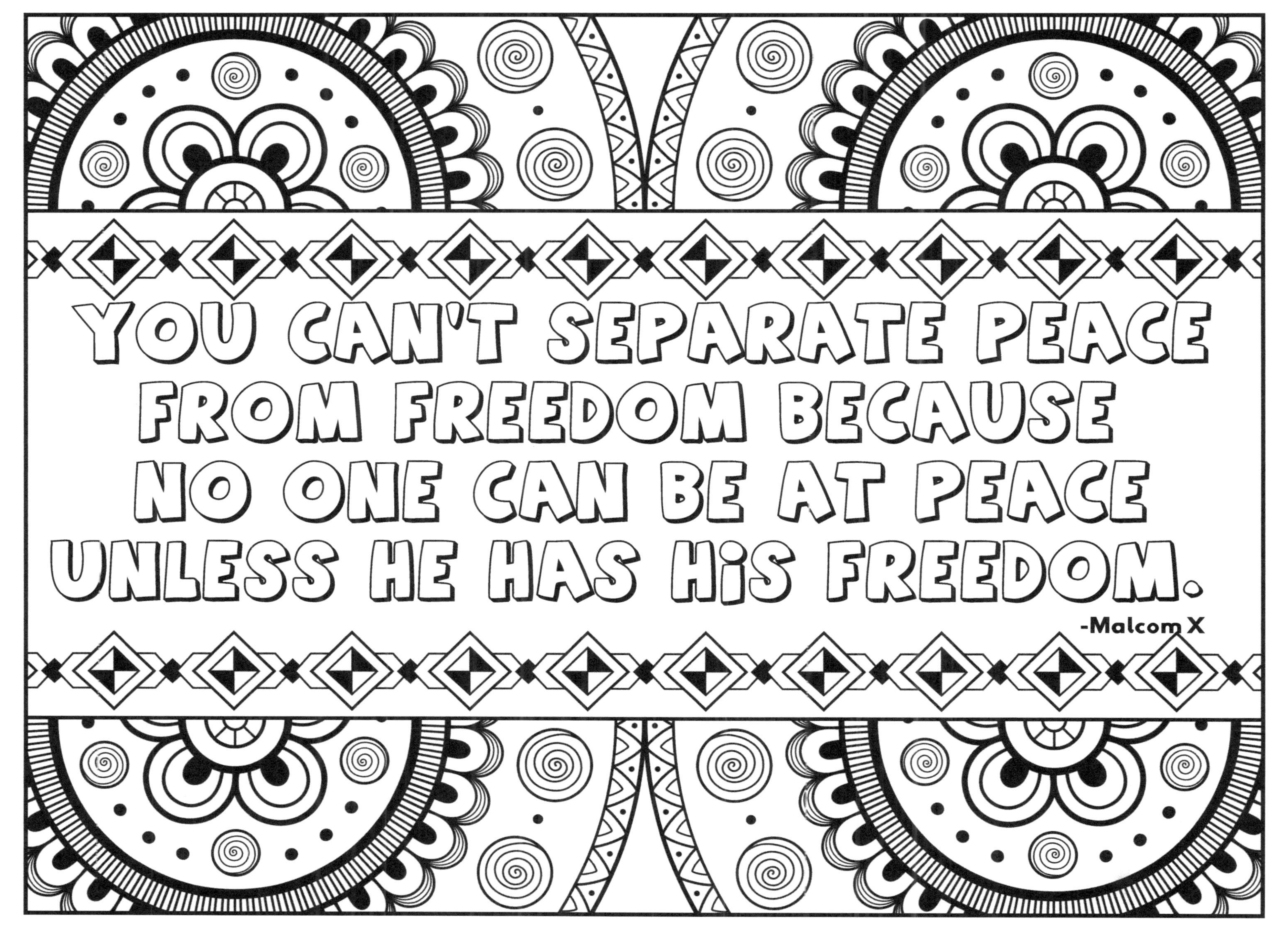

YOU CAN'T SEPARATE PEACE
FROM FREEDOM BECAUSE
NO ONE CAN BE AT PEACE
UNLESS HE HAS HIS FREEDOM.
-Malcom X

ACTIVISM
IS MY RENT
FOR LIVING
ON THE
PLANET
-Alice Walker

Positive
Action

CHANGE WILL NOT COME IF WE WAIT FOR SOME OTHER PERSON OR SOME OTHER TIME. WE ARE THE ONES WE'VE BEEN WAITING FOR. WE ARE THE CHANGE THAT WE SEEK.
-President Barack Obama

EQUAL
JUSTICE
UNDER
LAW

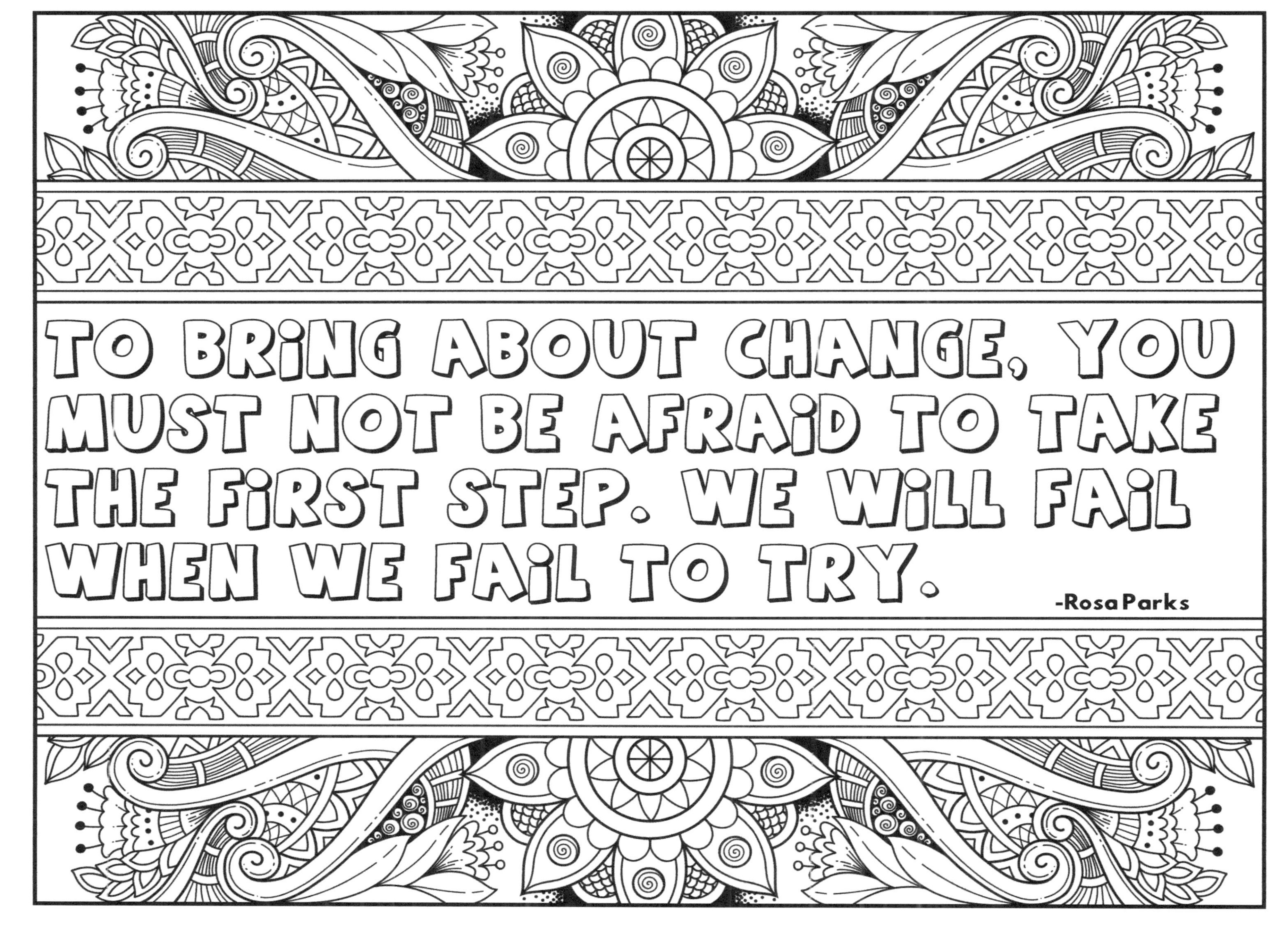

To bring about change, you must not be afraid to take the first step. We will fail when we fail to try.
-Rosa Parks

RACISM, Isn't Born,
IT IS TAUGHT

BLM

The eyes are useless when the mind is
BLIND

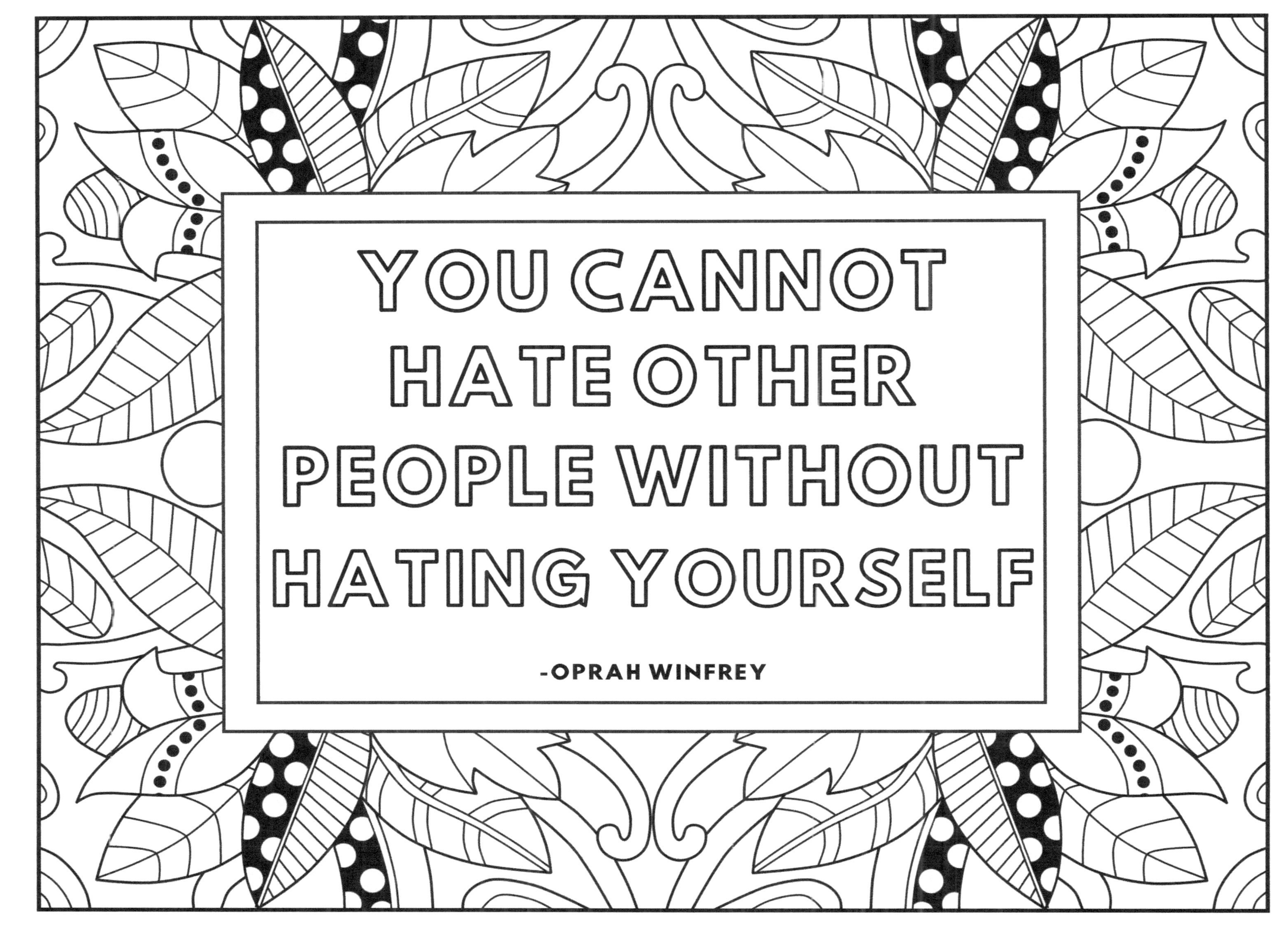

YOU CANNOT
HATE OTHER
PEOPLE WITHOUT
HATING YOURSELF
-OPRAH WINFREY

NO
JUSTiCE
NO
PEACE

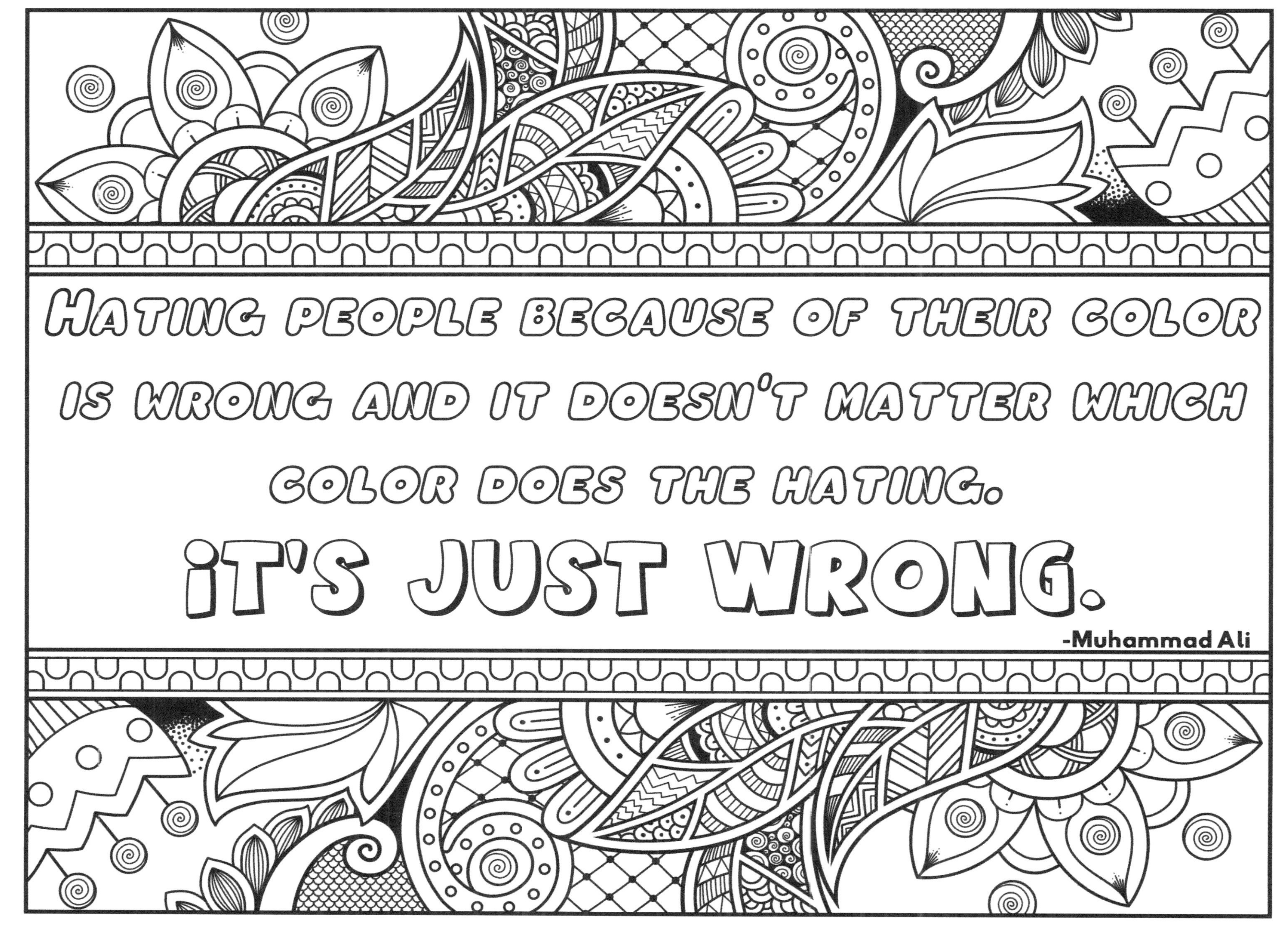

Hating people because of their color is wrong and it doesn't matter which color does the hating.
It's just wrong.
-Muhammad Ali

Achievement
has no
COLOR
-ABRAHAM LINCOLN

WE RISE
BY
LIFTING
OTHERS

WE ARE ONE
HUMAN
RACE

Not everything that is faced can be changed, but nothing can be changed until it is faced.
-JAMES BALDWIN

God is
LOVE
Not Hate

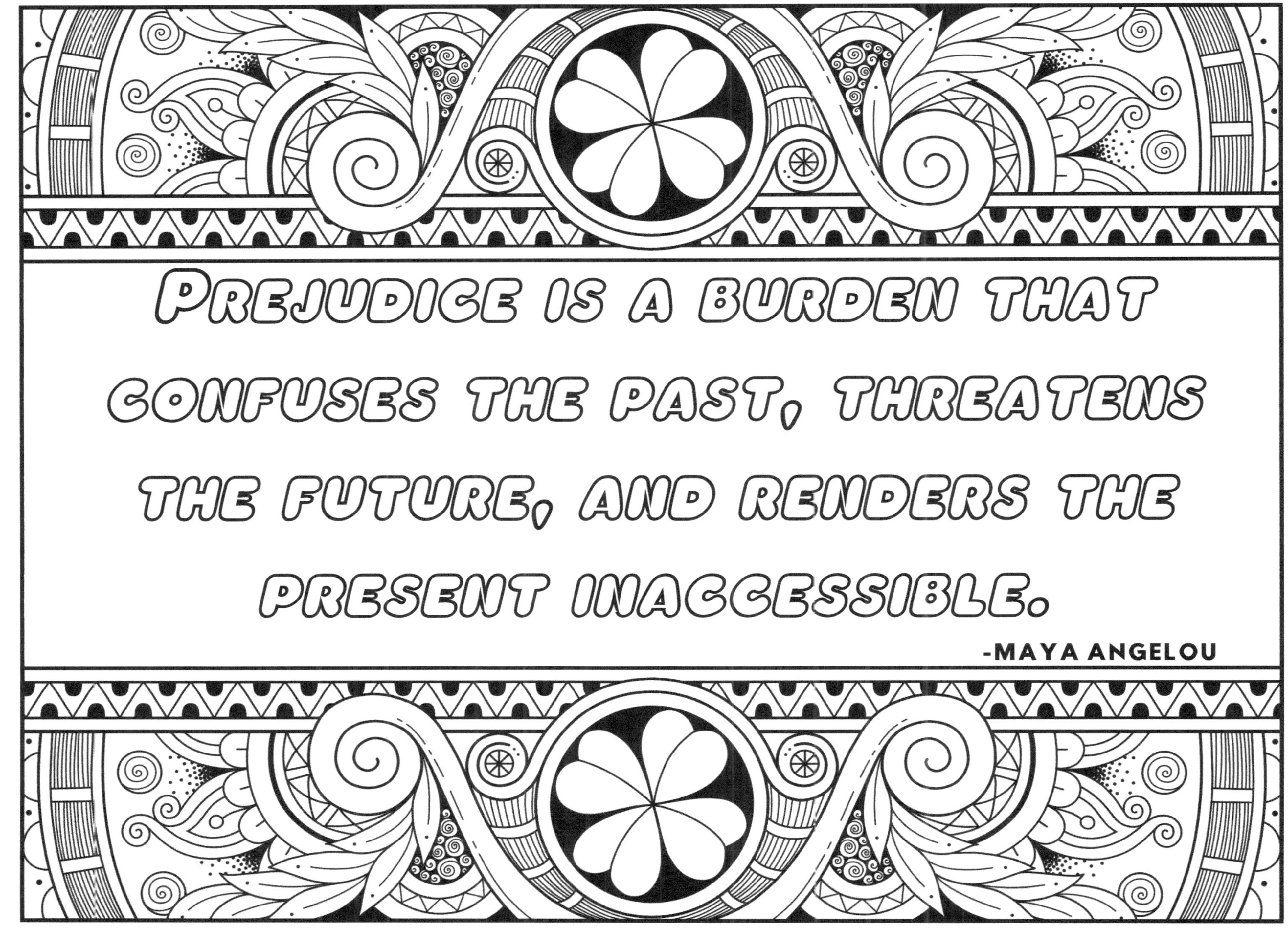

PREJUDICE IS A BURDEN THAT CONFUSES THE PAST, THREATENS THE FUTURE, AND RENDERS THE PRESENT INACCESSIBLE.
-MAYA ANGELOU

Injustice anywhere
is a threat to
Injustice everywhere
-DR. MARTIN LUTHER KING

MY HUMANITY
IS BOUND UP
IN YOURS,
FOR WE CAN
ONLY BE
HUMAN
TOGETHER.
-Desmond Tutu

EQUALITY

In this country, American means white. Everybody else has to hyphenate.
-TONI MORRISON

BLACK
LIVES
MATTER

The need for change bulldozed a road down the center of my mind.
-MAYA ANGELOU

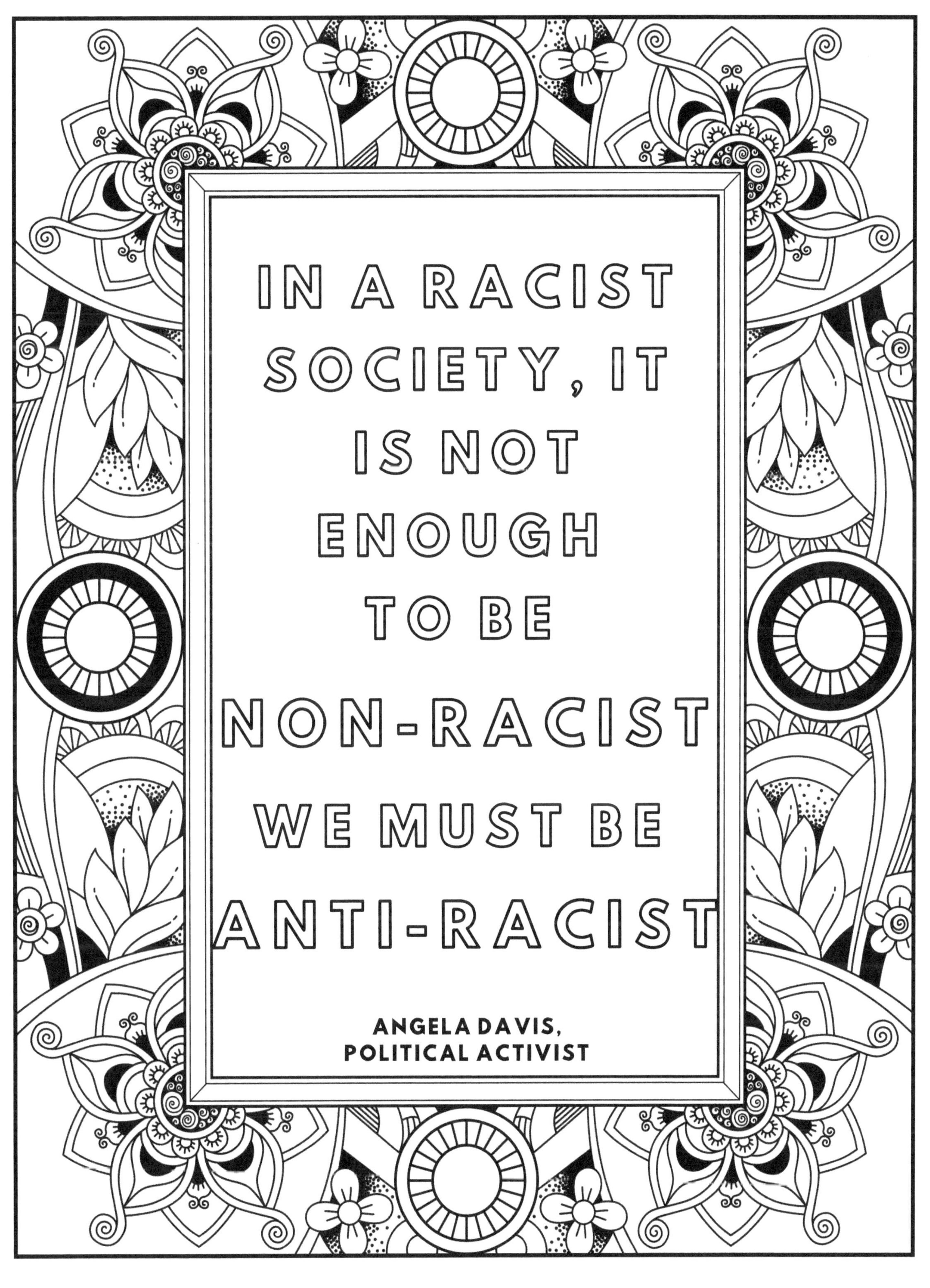

IN A RACIST SOCIETY, IT IS NOT ENOUGH TO BE NON-RACIST WE MUST BE ANTI-RACIST
ANGELA DAVIS, POLITICAL ACTIVIST